The Wings of My Soul

Poems

by

Alima Ravadi Quinn

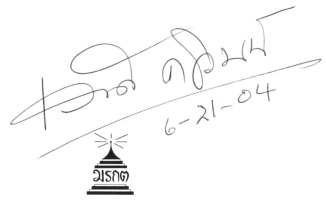

Emerald of Siam

With great appreciation

to my sister

Angela Sujitra

Arunthanes

for financing this book

For my children

Amy, Jim, Suzy,

Dara and Bill,

Grandchildren

Jared, Lee, Louis, Cara,

Mandalyn and Arthur

Contents

Foreword

When I need fabulous food I go to Alima Ravadi's restaurant, **The Emerald of Siam.** And when I am there I often read her poetry for nourishment. Her words, like her food, reflect a perfect blending of textures and flavors, one leading gently and brightly to the next. A bit of sweetness may be surrounded by a flashing of spicy fire. A subtle moist morsel may be held together by a crisp form of structure. Her food and her words offer delicate form and function which come together to create **Art.**

I believe **Art** is alive and creates change in the person who produces it as well as those who observe it. Art demands relationship with all its elements. By this criterion I define Alima Ravadi's collection of poetry as art. But here's the catch. If art demands relationship with the art as well as its creator, then one must recognize these tender words are merely the poet's appetizer. The poet herself is the entr'ee, the essence of the work is the dessert and the total relationship is an entire meal of Soul.

I would like to suggest a way to maximize your enjoyment of this book. After you have read all the poems written, then buy Alima Ravadi's other book, **The Joy of Thai Cooking.** Follow one of her recipes and replicate the fine cuisine. Then go to her restaurant and eat something she has cooked herself after she has meditated over the food as she prepared it. Note the **divine** difference. She has made a translation of common ingredients into food poetry. Then go back to your own kitchen and make the dish again. Now, take her poetry book to a quiet place for another read. Re-read her poems as simple recipes with basic ingredients and instructions for finding unconditional love, information on where and how to find the Divine, steps to experience positive life enhancing bliss, and how to turn the mundane into the omnipresent. Then do your day as a meditative offering of the heart. Note the **divine** difference.

As a writing teacher I work to teach my students how to get out of their own way to let the "Light of the Divine" transmit through their pens or keyboards. Alima Ravadi seems to be a conduit for the Divine. A critic might try to suggest that there is "nothing original" here and compare her words to poets like Rumi or other mystics. In simple agreement I would say, "Yes, of course, because **Truth is Truth.**" But I also believe that when the poet has a love affair with the **Divine Beloved** their reflections of Truth are much closer to the mark than those of us who stumble awkwardly outside the Radiant doors of Truth hoping for a mere glimpse of the Sacred.

Read these poems like mantras, chant them as prayer, sing them, drum them, fly them, drink them with tea. Hear in them the World. Hear in them the Heart. Hear in them the Child. Hear in them the Mother. Hear in them the Soul. Hear in them the Silence. Hear in them the simple elegant Truth. Then wait quietly for your personal invitation to have a sweet meal of Love at the table of the **Divine Beloved.**

Vali Hawkins Mitchell, PhD
Author of Dr. Vali's Survival Guide: Tips for the Journey
November 1998

Spiritual Awareness

Spiritual awareness
Begins with unlearning of human habits.

❦ ❦ ❦

The mind always speaks to you without invitation.
The heart will not speak until you open it.

❦ ❦ ❦

Your mind has many teachers.
Your heart has only one,
And it is you.

❦ ❦ ❦

You may structure anything you want
Except your heart.
It was already created to flow with the universe.

❦ ❦ ❦

When You Have A Question

When you have a question
ask your mind.

When you want an answer
ask your heart.

🌀 🌀 🌀

If you want God's help
Surrender!

If you want to find yourself
Awaken!

If you want to connect with the universe
Open your heart!

🌀 🌀 🌀

I Was Created

I was created.
First the spirit and body,
My mind came later.

🥀 🥀 🥀

When you love yourself
You will love the world
And everything in it.

🥀 🥀 🥀

When my friend told me
What a wonderful person I was,
My lips said, "Thank you,"
But my heart said,
"Wait until you see my Creator."
"You will find me only a drop of the ocean."

🥀 🥀 🥀

Illusion and Reality

Illusion and Reality are identical twins.
Until you can define one
You cannot identify the other.

❧ ❧ ❧

Perfection can only be found in our inner world.
When once we find it
We will find the flexibility of the outer world.

❧ ❧ ❧

Our inner world is created by God.
The outer world is created by our minds.

❧ ❧ ❧

Fear and Love

Where there is fear there are rules.

Where there are rules there is punishment.

Where there is punishment there is suffering.

Where there is suffering there is death.

Where there is love there is freedom.

Where there is freedom there is forgiveness.

Where there is forgiveness there is healing.

Where there is healing there is joy and peace.

I Love

I love life *but I love God more.*

I love food *but I love my body more.*

I love my mind *but I love silence more.*

I love money *but I love spiritual freedom more.*

I love happiness *but I love joy and peace more.*

I love education *but I love self-knowledge more.*

I love individualism *but I love wholeness more.*

I love illusion *but I love my soul more.*

I love receiving *but I love giving more.*

I love myself *but I love children more.*

I love my family *but I love the global family more.*

❀ ❀ ❀

The Divine Moments

My Beloved,

May I borrow Your body for one moment
So that I may feel Your love?

May I borrow Your eyes for one moment
So that I may see the perfection of Your creation?

May I borrow Your ears for one moment
So that I may hear Your wisdom in silence?

May I borrow Your mind for one moment
So that I may learn humility?

May I borrow Your compassion for one moment
So that I may forgive myself and others?

May I borrow Your tears for one moment
So that I may experience the joy of Your presence?

May I borrow Your smile for one moment
So that I may appreciate Your frienship?

May I borrow Your laughter for one moment
So that I may not fear enjoying life?

May I borrow Your breath for one moment
So that I may trust You for eternity?

Attention

When I was a child
I needed my mother's attention.

When I was a youth
I wanted my friend's attention.

When I was a maiden
I desired my prince's attention.

When I became a woman
I paid attention to myself
And I found the king waiting for my attention.

A Human Quest for Enlightenment

Because of our ignorance we search for wisdom.

Because of our suffering we search for compassion.

Because of our fear we search for love.

Because of our pain we search for healing.

Because of our loneliness we search for happiness.

Because of our emptiness we search for wholeness.

Because of our restless minds we search for creativity.

Because of our attachment we search for freedom.

Because of our illusion we search for truth.

Because of our separation we search for union.

Because of our union with God we end our search.

Our spiritual journey with Joy and Peace begins.

🥀 🥀 🥀

Awaken!

There is no greater wealth than
Awakening in the wholeness of the heart.

There is no greater security than
Awakening in the womb of the universe.

There is no greater abundance than
Awakening in the wisdom of the earth.

There is no greater joy than
Awakening in the arms of the divine presence.

The Conversation

Why am I so happy being nothing?
I asked.
    Because you are everything to Me,
    I heard.

Why do I always get disappointed when I try to teach someone? I asked.
    Because there is only one Teacher, and it is not you,
    I heard.

Why do my children not follow my wishes?
I asked.
    Because they are following My clues,
    I heard.

Why do I no longer desire to become rich?
I asked.
    Because you have found enough oil to light your eternal path, I heard.

Why do I no longer experience fear and pain?
I asked.
    Because they became My compassion.
    I heard.

Why is all I see in the world LOVE?
I asked.
    Because you are seeing it through My eyes,
    I heard.

In This Lifetime

In this lifetime
No need to wait until next.

When you find yourself in Hell
You will find devils following you everywhere.

When you find yourself in Limbo
You will find good and evil in different forms.

When you find yourself in Heaven
You will find angels assisting you without fail.

🌹 🌹 🌹

When I Kiss A Rose

When I kiss a rose
I kiss myself.

When I love a child
I love myself.

When I hold a friend
I hold myself.

When I hold an enemy
God holds me.

Message To The World

Each child is given a new message to the world.
Don't give him yours,
But listen to his.
It can be a message of peace to your heart.

❧ ❧ ❧

Love is a universal language
Spoken through human hearts.
It became complicated
By the communication of human minds.

❧ ❧ ❧

Human Mind

A fearful mind is a house of ignorance.

A busy mind is a house of survivors.

A wandering mind is a house of seekers.

A quiet mind is a house of faith.

Healings

Food heals hunger.

Love heals loneliness.

Intelligence heals jealousy.

Trust heals anxiety.

Forgiveness heals anger.

Silence heals the mind.

Inner growth heals fear.

Divine love heals emptiness.

Spiritual freedom heals suffering.

Compassion heals all humanity.

🌹 🌹 🌹

When I Found

I stopped feeling sorry for myself
When I found
Learning is a way of life.

> I stopped following my mind
> When I found
> Silence reveals my path.

I stopped discriminating
When I found
Unity of diversity is the Creator's purpose.

> I stopped judging
> When I found
> God is unconditional love.

I stopped making plans
When I found
Inspiration is more fun and meaningful.

> I stopped looking for what I want
> When I found
> Wholeness with the Universe.

I started nurturing myself
When I found
I am the loving child of God.

> I started enjoying life
> When I found
> My cosmic duty.

I started giving with pure joy
When I found
Prosperity in my heart.

Until

The spiritual journey began with the heart

Until

It was trapped in the comfort and discomfort of the body

Until

It was intoxicated by the illusion of the mind

Until

It was challenged by the reasons of the intellect

Until

It found its way home, awakened with wisdom.

🌸 🌸 🌸

Which Path Are You On?

A human path is the path of the body and the mind.
A spiritual path is the path of the heart.
Which path are you on?

A human path is the path of right and wrong.
A spiritual path is a path of acceptance.
Which path are you on?

A human path is the path of reward and punishment.
A spiritual path is a path of giving and forgiving.
Which path are you on?

A human path is the path of individualism.
A spiritual path is a path of wholeness.
Which path are you on?

Teach Yourself

When your child feels lonely
Hold him to your heart
And teach yourself friendship.

        When your child shows anxiety
        Hold him to your heart
        And teach yourself trust.

When your child experiences hatred
Hold him to your heart
And teach yourself tolerance.

        When your child is starting to judge
        Hold him to your heart
        And teach yourself acceptance.

When your child hangs on to anger
Hold him to your heart
And teach yourself forgiveness.

        When your child is afraid
        Hold him to your heart
        And remind yourself that

You are at home with unconditional love.

🌹 🌹 🌹

When I Found My Heart

My heart is grounded like the earth
that contains and embraces all lives.

My heart flows like water that sustains
and purifies all things.

My heart moves like the air that expands
and integrates the breath of all lives.

My heart is burning with compassion like fire
that raises all humanity to one conscious love.

Full Cycle

I didn't know I was in this world
Until I realized I had a body.
All I knew was, I had a heart to love.

    I didn't know I had a mind
    Until I got caught doing something not quite right.
    All I knew was, I had a heart to love.

I didn't know life would be so strange and difficult
Until I left the bosom of my family.
All I knew was, I had a heart to love.

    I didn't know there were so many religions
    Until some of them claimed me.
    All I knew was, I had a heart to love.

I didn't know I had so much to sacrifice
Until I had a family of my own.
All I knew was, I had a heart to love.

    I didn't know there were so many challenges
    Until I followed my duties to their ends.
    All I knew was, I had a heart to love.

I didn't know there were such things as joy and peace
Until I held my newborn grand-daughter in my arms.
All I knew was, love had embraced my heart.

    🌹 🌹 🌹

Because I Know

I feel safe because I know
I am in the arms of the Divine love.

       I feel strong and confident because I know
       I am nurtured by Mother Earth's wisdom.

I am flexible because I know
Diversity is a fun way to live.

       I feel free because I know
       I was created with unconditional love.

I feel whole because I know
My creator intended me to be.

The Unity of Ideals

Art expresses creation.

Science explains natural laws.

Philosophy explains life.

Music orchestrates the rhythm of the Cosmos.

Poetry speaks for the heart.

Religion maintains hope.

Technology enhances life.

Spirituality transforms human hearts.

Peace unites all beings in one conscious love.

☘ ☘ ☘

Love Sustains Life

Love sustains life.
Peace sustains love.
Compassion sustains peace.

❧ ❧ ❧

Each of us is an instrument
to express different aspects
of God's love

❧ ❧ ❧

The soul seeks to express
itself best through love,
harmony and beauty,
which are hidden in human hearts.

❧ ❧ ❧

Learn with your mind, but
practice with your heart.

❧ ❧ ❧

The Journey

Life without purpose is a process.
Suffering continues.

      Life with purpose is the end of process.
      Suffering ceases.

Spiritual life continues.
Inner joy and healing power begin.

           🌹 🌹 🌹

Open Your Heart

On a sunny day
Open your heart.
Your spirit will soar to join the birds
To view the world.

On a rainy day
Open your heart.
Your spirit will go under the ground by the roots of the tree
To thank mother earth for the day.

On a stormy day
Open your heart.
Your spirit will go under the sea
And rest for a while.

On a quiet day
Open your heart.
Your spirit will find the world
Was created with love, harmony and beauty.

Pleasure

When you find pleasure in friendship
Friends will find you.

When you find pleasure in giving
Abundance will supply you.

When you find pleasure in caring
Healing power will be with you.

When you find pleasure in learning your natural gift
Inspiration will motivate you.

When you find pleasure in service
Peace and compassion will escort you.

When you find pleasure in Divine Knowledge
Nature will speak to you.

When you find pleasure in Divine Love
You are safe at the center of the Universe.

Heaven And Earth

My father is a shining light from heaven.
My mother is a sacred gift from the earth.

   My father gave me his global vision.
   My mother gave me her earthly wisdom.

My father taught me courage by his failure.
My mother gave me courage by her liberal womanhood.

   My father taught me acceptance by his tolerance.
   My mother's unconditional love made me feel accepted.

My father's vision lighted my path.
My mother's wisdom nurtured my confidence.

   My father taught me freedom of the mind.
   My mother taught me the power of an open heart.

When my father passed away
He left me with a beautiful path to continue.

   When my mother left her body
   She left a gift of wholeness in my heart.

        🌹   🌹   🌹

When You Are Ready

When you are ready to be a student
You are your own teacher.

When you are ready to be healed
You are your own healer.

When you are ready to be loved
You are already loved.

When you are ready to be peaceful
You are already at peace with yourself.

🌹 🌹 🌹

The Beauty And The Beast

Intellect talks about love and relationship.
The heart speaks about compassion and connectedness.

Intellect loves freedom.
The heart prefers to surrender.

Intellect has hope.
The heart has faith.

Intellect knows right and wrong.
The heart has no room for them.

Intellect makes changes.
The heart grows and expands.

Intellect learns how to succeed.
The heart learns how to accept failure.

Intellect seeks pleasure of the world.
The heart seeks pleasure in service.

Intellect cultivates individualism.
The heart maintains wholeness.

Intellect's destination is with this world.
The heart rests in Cosmic Love.

❀ ❀ ❀

Signs

Loving is a sign of security.

Learning is a sign of growth.

Creativity is a sign of intelligence.

Happiness is a sign of satisfaction.

Illness and loss are signs of spiritual need.

Gratitude is a sign of maturity.

Self-discipline is a sign of wisdom.

Giving is a sign of fulfillment.

Compassion is a sign of peace.

Service from the heart is the sign of wholeness.

❀ ❀ ❀

Love

Human love is a journey of the mind and body.
Divine love is a journey of the spirit.

        Human love limits by fear.
        Divine love expands by security.

Human love limits by discrimination.
Divine love expands by diversity.

        Human love limits by intellect.
        Divine love expands by wisdom.

Human love limits by right and wrong.
Divine love expands by acceptance.

        Human love limits by immaturity.
        Divine love expands by gratitude.

Human love limits by suffering.
Divine love expands by sacrifice.

        Human love ceases with the body.
        Divine love continues with the spirit.

Be Aware!

Your mind and body always mess things up
While you are asleep.
Awaken.

🥀 🥀 🥀

Your mind is like a river that never stops running:
Your heart is like the ocean that rejects no river.
When the mind reaches the heart
It stops running and dances with the heart's desire.

🥀 🥀 🥀

Nature will speak to you only
When your mind stops talking.

When the mind speaks
Nature waits silently for its turn.

When nature speaks
The mind trembles.

🥀 🥀 🥀

Because Of You
For My Children

Because of you
I was created

      Because of you
      I was taught unconditional love

Because of you
I was taught self-sacrifice

      Because of you
      I was taught individualism

Because of you
I was taught trustworthiness

      Because of you
      I was taught freedom of the spirit

Because of you
I was taught to let go

      Because of you
      I learned my purpose in life

Without You
For Alim Quinn

Without you
I would never be weaned from my parents.

    Without you
    I would never challenge a larger world.

Without you
I would never explore my potential.

    Without you
    I would never find my courage.

Without you
I would never find myself.

    Without you
    I would never find my cosmic duty.

Without you
I would never learn compassion.

    Without you
    I would never find wholeness within me.

🌹 🌹 🌹

Freedom

Which freedom are you seeking?

Mechanical freedom is structured by the mind.
Spiritual freedom flows through the heart.

Mechanical freedom is limited by logic.
Spiritual freedom is boundless.

Mechanical freedom is the fruit of intelligence.
Spiritual freedom is the fruit of self-realization.

Mechanical freedom seeks pleasure with the mind.
Spiritual freedom seeks pleasure with the heart.

Mechanical freedom is the friend of attachment.
Spiritual freedom is detachment.

Mechanical freedom frees you from poverty.
Spiritual freedom frees you from suffering.

Mechanical freedom ends with the mind.
Spiritual freedom continues eternally.

Which freedom have you found?

🙐 🙐 🙐

Center of the Universe

When you are at the center of the Universe

Your heart no longer hold secrets;

Your mind no longer judges, but creates in silence:

Your breath is in rhythm with the ocean waves;

Your insight is the depth of the ocean;

Your body manifests itself as a temple of God.

🍥 🍥 🍥

The Masters

When I read the Scripture
I found unconditional love on the Cross.

       When I read Buddha's teachings
       I found the power of the mind.

When I read Rumi's poems
I found myself swimming in the ocean of love.

Being a Child

When I was an infant
I was a child to my parents.
I knew.

        When I was a student
        I was a child to my teacher.
        I learned.

When I was an adult
I was a child to my town.
I behaved.

        When I became a parent
        I was a mother to my child.
        I sacrificed.

When I became a woman
I was the mother of my own self.
I relearned.

        When I became a grandmother
        I was initiated as mother of the earth.
        I found myself.

🌹 🌹 🌹

If Only I Knew
A sacred union

If only I knew you were with me when I was a child,
I would never need my parents.

If only I knew you were with me when I was a student,
I would never need my teachers.

If only I knew you were with me when I wanted a friend,
I would never need to look for one.

If only I knew you were with me when I raised my children,
I would never experience fear and pain.

If only I knew you were with me when I lost my parents,
I would never have to grieve.

If only I knew you were with me when I was sick,
I would never need a healer.

If only I knew you were with me when I searched for you,
I would never walk in the dark.

Now I can let go of all my fear and pain
And I am not afraid if you decide to take away my breath
Because I know you are with me for eternity.

🥀 🥀 🥀

New Year Day 1997

A Happy New Year.

A continuation of new beginning.

A reflection of the past.

A capture of a new moment.

A resolution of trust in the future.

A prayer for world's peace.

An awareness of one conscious Love among us.

🌀 🌀 🌀

Man

Fortunate man is controlled by his fortune.

Unfortunate man blames his past karma.

Intellectual man is influenced by his knowledge.

Wise man is guided by his wisdom.

Compassion

Let compassion direct your love
      Like the sun giving breath to all beings.

Let compassion direct your mind
      Like the river searching for the ocean.

Let compassion direct your desire
      For love, harmony and beauty.

Let compassion direct your will
      To harmonize with the cosmic evolution.

🥀 🥀 🥀

How I Live

When I live with my body
I am always hungry for love.

When I live with my mind
I often live in the past and worry about the future.

When I live with my spirit
I always find myself in the present moment.

When I live with my heart
I find myself in love with the Universe.

☙ ☙ ☙

God Creates

God creates the world with compassion in silence.
Man creates his world by his thoughts and emotions.

❦ ❦ ❦

A positive mind will help you get what you want.

A quiet mind will help you find who you are and find yourself most wanted.

❦ ❦ ❦

Individualism frees your mind.
Wholeness frees your spirit.

❦ ❦ ❦

Human behavior is the complexity of the mind.
Look down one foot deeper;
You will find the simplicity of the heart.

❦ ❦ ❦

Free Youself

Free your inner child.
Your pain will free you.

Free your anger.
Your forgiveness will free you.

Free your thoughts.
Your mind will free you.

Free your intellect.
Your wisdom will free you.

Free your individual self.
Your wholeness will free you.

Free your conditional love.
The Universe will free you with compassion.

🌀 🌀 🌀

When You Take Care of Youself

When you take care of yourself
You are taking care of all of God's creation.

When you take care of a child
You are taking care of the environment.

When you transform yourself
You are evolving with the Cosmic love.

Cosmic Duty

Radiate your love
As the rays of the sun reaching the earth.

Radiate your faith
As the bird trusting the sky.

Radiate your compassion
As the ocean rejecting no rivers.

Radiate your gratitude
As the spring flowers greeting their Creator.

Radiate your patience
As the winter trees waiting for the spring.

Radiate your peace
As the silence of the moon
Reflecting on still water.

🌼 🌼 🌼

Thank You God

Thank you God
For being the earth for me to stand on.

Thank you God
For being the water to sustain my body.

Thank you God
For being the fire to kindle my heart.

Thank you God
For being my breath to keep the rhythm of the Universe.

Thank you God
For your compassion that holds me for eternity.

🌹 🌹 🌹

Inner Orchard

Suffering is the fruit of ignorance.

Pain is the fruit of growth.

Happiness is the fruit of creativity.

Detachment is the fruit of spiritual maturity.

Faith is the fruit of compassion and peace.

Lake O'Hara

Oh! Lake O'Hara, I love you.
Your beauty has brought our bodies together
to experience God's love and compassion.

Oh! Lake O'Hara, I praise you.
Your tranquility has brought our minds
to continue God's creation.

Oh! Lake O'Hara, I adore you.
Your solitude has brought our spirits
to maintain God's will and sovereignty.

Oh! Lake O'Hara, I will always hold you in my heart
because your perfection has brought our souls
to sustain oneness of humanity.

Lake O'Hara Sufi Camp 1997

🌸 🌸 🌸

Dara

You are the Star of all stars in the sky.

Your smile is the beauty of all spring flowers.

Your music is the sound of the universe

Your love and mine are one in eternity.

Happy birthday 11/30/1997
With love from your Mom

Just Be

Just be a loving master to your body and mind.

Just be a loving student to your inner teacher.

Just be a loving servant to your heart.

Just be a loving child to God.

You will find yourself back in paradise.

🌸 🌸 🌸

My Grandchild: The Reflection of the Universe

Your eyes are stars that enhance the dark sky.

Your smile is the gentleness of the moon.

Your openness is flowers in Spring.

Your laugh brightens my heart.

Your cries always awaken my soul.

Your every body movement leads me into the cosmic dance.

I feel at home with you in my arms.

An Invitation

Come and visit my paradise.
When you need to grieve
I will be your tears to replace what you lost.

      Come and visit my paradise.
      When you are angry with the world
      You will see what you saw was a false picture.

Come and visit my paradise.
When you are lonely
My longing for you will fill your emptiness.

      Come and visit my paradise.
      When you are in fear or in pain
      My compassion will make you whole.

Come and visit my paradise.
When you are at peace with yourself
You will find you and I are one with all beings.

      🌹 🌹 🌹

A Reunion

My son returned home.
He needed me
To fix his wings as I had with his sister's,
I thought

      He was happy to be home.
      My heart filled with delight
      And surprise to hear
      That he had come home to fix his nest.

He didn't know
I fixed the nest after he was gone
Nor did I know
He strengthened his wings before his return.

      Now he is home
      With his strong wings
      And ready to soar
      From his healthy nest.

🌹 🌹 🌹

Opportunity

Opening your mind is an opportunity of
Creating Beauty.

Opening your heart is an opportunity of
Creating Love.

Opening to your spirit is an opportunity to
Dance with your soul.

Just Love Me

I am very fragile like a child.
I can only take one step at a time.
Do not push me or pull me.
Encourage me if you can; if you can't,
Just love me.

I am very new to the world.
When I am lost and ask for help
Don't tell me what I should have done.
Help me if you can; if you can't,
Just love me.

My emotions are my birthright,
So I may experience my human limitation.
When I am in fear or in pain,
Hold me or listen to me if you can; if you can't,
Just love me.

Innocence is my divine nature.
When I enjoy what I like and what I do,
Don't interrupt and take it away from me.
If you do, both of us will need to be healed.
Just loving me is not enough.

🌀 🌀 🌀

Christmas Gifts

The best Christmas gift to your child is to remember :

Each child was born with a Divine message.
Listen!

Each child was born with unconditional love.
Nurture!

Each child was born with a gift.
Recognize!

Each child was born unique.
Accept!

Each child was born with the responsibility to know him/herself.
Encourage!

Each child was born with free will.
Respect!

Each child was born with a Cosmic duty.
Let go and trust the process!

❀ ❀ ❀

We Share
A Reflection on Diversity

You and I walk different paths
    But we share the same destination.

You and I live in different forms
    But we share the same elements.

You and I have different wills
    But we share the same bliss of God.

You and I have different desires
    But we share the same need for compassion.

You and I experience different fears and pains
    But we share the same roots of healing.

You and I have different gifts of intelligence
    But we share the same privilege of being human.

You and I have different mothers
    But we share the same abundance of Mother Earth.

You and I have different faiths and traditions
    But we share the same Spirit of Love and Guidance.

You and I create different illusions to make sense out of life
    But we share the same Truth that brings joy and peace.

🌹 🌹 🌹

Wisdom of Health
A Journey Into Wholeness

Tune your breath and body until
You become one rhythm with nature.

Educate your mind until
You can create and communicate in silence.

Discipline your will until
You can agree with God's will.

Listen to your desire deeply until
You can hear it from the heart.

Nurture and expand your heart until
You can embrace all beings with compassion.

Cultivate your patience until
You have faith to witness the process.

Transcend all your emotions until
You can flow with the cosmic evolution.

❦ ❦ ❦

Self - Satisfaction

Love, food and pleasure are satisfaction of the body.

Creativity in silence is satisfaction of the mind.

Freedom of each moment is satisfaction of the spirit.

Being one with the Universe is satisfaction of the heart.

A Special Invitation from the Author

Alima Ravadi is available to come to you and perform a live reading of her poetry. This may be exactly what you need to:

Rekindle your spirit.

Raise funds for your organization, charity, or for a special purpose.

Experience a moment of spiritual and aesthetic transformation.

If you would like more information about hosting a poetry reading, or if you would like to order more copies of "Wings of My Soul," order Ravadi's cookbook, "Joy of Thai Cooking," or just send your greetings, please call or write to:

The Emerald of Siam
1314 Jadwin Avenue
Richland, Washington 99352
USA

(509) 946-9328
or
(509) 946-2595

e-mail: rrgarry@urx.com